I (HEART)
Art

Wisdom With
Understanding
is Better
Than Rubies

Lurine Karon Greenberg
Fine Arts Collection

I (HEART) Art

ART WE LOVE FROM
THE METROPOLITAN MUSEUM OF ART

ABRAMS BOOKS FOR YOUNG READERS, NEW YORK

I (HEART) Art

If you are reading this, then very likely you too (Heart) Art! The term "art" covers a wide range of media and subjects. Art can be painted on paper, board, or ceramics; it can be sculpted, collaged, or printed. Within these pages you will discover some of the masterpieces from The Metropolitan Museum of Art as well as lesser-known works. Many of them are displayed in the Museum's galleries.

People who (Heart) art vary as much as the artwork itself. There are no restrictions to appreciating art. You don't need to study art in school. You don't need to attend lectures or watch documentaries and films. These things will enhance your understanding of an individual artwork or of an artist or movement, but you know you (Heart) art the moment you see a work that moves you. (And it is OK to not [Heart] a work of art, even if everyone else seems to!)

This book is arranged by themes. The art was created at different times in history and by people from around the globe, reflecting their diverse cultural and artistic heritage. *I (HEART) Art* is a book you can come back to again and again, because a piece of art can mean something different to you each time you look at it, depending on your mood and what is going on around you.

Within these pages, we hope you find art that you (Heart)!

Who doesn't (Heart) to play?

Running feet and splashing hands,

Blowing bubbles and bouncing balls,

Flying kites and gliding skates,

There are so many ways to play.

I (HEART)
Play

Jean Monet on His Hobby Horse

detail, 1872, by **CLAUDE MONET**. French. Oil on canvas.

4

Boating Party with Children Swimming

late eighteenth century, by **KITAGAWA UTAMARO**. Japanese. DIptych of polychrome woodblock prints; ink and color on paper.

H. O. Havemeyer Collection, Bequest of Mrs. H. O. Havemeyer, 1929.

7

Manuel Osorio Manrique de Zuñiga

1787–88, by
GOYA (FRANCISCO DE
GOYA Y LUCIENTES).

Spanish. Oil on canvas.

The Jules Bache Collection,
1949.

8

Seated Ballplayer

first century BCE
through third century CE.
Ameca-Etzatlán (Mexico).
Ceramic.

Gift of The Andrall and Joanne
Pearson Collection, 2005.

9

The Children of Nathan Starr

1835, by **AMBROSE ANDREWS**. American. Oil on canvas.

Gift of Nina Howell Starr, in memory of Nathan Comfort Starr (1896–1981), 1987.

Soap Bubbles

c. 1733–34, by **JEAN SIMÉON CHARDIN**. French. Oil on canvas.
Wentworth Fund, 1949.

Pool Parlor

1942, by **JACOB LAWRENCE**. American.

Watercolor and gouache on paper.

Arthur Hoppock Hearn Fund, 1942. © 2019 The Jacob and Gwendolyn Knight Lawrence Foundation, Seattle / Artists Rights Society (ARS), New York.

15

The Swing

detail, late eighteenth century, by **HUBERT ROBERT**. French.
Oil on canvas.

Gift of J. Pierpont Morgan, 1917.

The Chess Players

c. 1475, by **LIBERALE DA VERONA**.
Italian. Tempera on wood.

Maitland F. Griggs Collection,
Bequest of Maitland F. Griggs, 1943.

Snap the Whip

1872, by WINSLOW HOMER. American. Oil on canvas.

Gift of Christian A. Zabriskie, 1950.

21

Steeplechase

1929, by **MILTON AVERY**. American. Oil on canvas.

Kite Flying

c. 1766, by **SUZUKI HARUNOBU**. Japanese.
Polychrome woodblock print; ink and color on paper.
Gift of Estate of Samuel Isham, 1914.

25

The Card Players

detail, 1890–92, by **PAUL CÉZANNE**. French. Oil on canvas.

Bequest of Stephen C. Clark, 1960.

Skating on the Wissahickon

1875, by JOHAN MENGELS CULVERHOUSE.

American. Oil on canvas.

Purchase, Rogers, Morris K. Jesup and Maria DeWitt Jesup Funds, and Charles and Anita Blatt Gift, 1974.

I (HEART)
Sports

Who doesn't (Heart) sports?

Running races and swinging mallets,

Wrestling stances and fencing feints,

Sliding bases and training ropes,

There are so many sports to choose.

***The Sumo Wrestlers Takaneyama
Yoichiemon and Sendagawa Kichigorō***

detail, c. 1790–93, by **KATSUSHIKA HOKUSAI**. Japanese.
Polychrome woodblock print; ink and color on paper.

The Francis Lathrop Collection, Purchase, Frederick C. Hewitt Fund, 1911.

Race Horses

c. 1885–88, by
EDGAR DEGAS. French.
Pastel on wood.

The Walter H. and Leonore
Annenberg Collection, Gift
of Walter H. and Leonore
Annenberg, 1999, Bequest of
Walter H. Annenberg, 2002.

Fencing Master

from the Occupations
of Women series (N502)
for Frishmuth's Tobacco
Company, 1889. American.
Commercial color
lithograph.

The Jefferson R. Burdick
Collection, Gift of Jefferson
R. Burdick.

36

Terracotta Panathenaic prize amphora

c. 366/365 BCE., attributed to a painter of the **KITTOS GROUP**. Greek. Terracotta; black-figure.

Fletcher Fund, 1956.

NATIONAL LEAGUE PLAYER #25
WILLIE MAYS
OUTFIELD
NEW YORK GIANTS

Born: Westfield, Ala., May 6, '31
Height: 5-11   **Weight:** 170
Bats: Right   **Throws:** Right

The return of Willie from his hitch in the Army bodes good things for the 1954 Giants. When Willie joined the team in 1951,—after hitting .477 for 35 games in Minneapolis — the Giants weren't doing so well. However, as all fans know, they wound up the year with a pennant. Willie loves to play ball, and his fielding is wonderful. He once caught a ball on the run in deep center at the Polo Grounds, whirled and threw a perfect strike to the plate to catch a man trying to score from third after the catch. This was in a vital game with Brooklyn in 1951.

Willie Mays

from the Major League All Star series (T234), 1954. Issued by Red
Man Chewing Tobacco. American. Commercial color lithograph.

"Siyavush Plays Polo before Afrasiyab", Folio 180v from the Shahnama (Book of Kings) of Shah Tahmasp

c. 1525–30, painting attributed to **QASIM IBN 'ALI**, from the book by Abu'l Qasim Firdausi. Iranian. Opaque watercolor, ink, silver, and gold on paper.

Gift of Arthur A. Houghton Jr., 1970.

همیکان بازی قیصر
مرد اَنَد بازی

همی خاک با آسمان کشتهاند
او کوبسته چندیدمیدان زتاب
پراده فروش بلیران با
جو کوی بازار اَنَشت نگر
او کوبسه بنزد بیاوش ئی
پیوخنن کوی ئی قیّ تست

خروش تیّ ترمیدان نهات
او آواز صبح و دُمّکر ئی
نگکنَد کوسه کیّ میدان نهان
پیبارکوسه نزمیدان زی
وکرز دخانخ نن میدان زی
بیاوش بازل می بره دوکوا

بازلِ بُرکیخت اسب نزد
بریانسکنه اَنجبه شدنامبید
بیاوش فروش میدان بای نکوس

یباوش بازل احبان نن نبد
او بنمود پس ثمریار بلند
پراده فروش میدان بای نکوس

وزان پس بخوبکان وکار کرد
خبان شکر کبان مه دیدار کرد

Harmony in Yellow and Gold: The Gold Girl—Connie Gilchrist

c. 1876–77, by JAMES MCNEILL WHISTLER. American. Oil on canvas.

Gift of George A. Hearn, 1911.

Boy with Baseball

c. 1925, by **GEORGE LUKS**. American. Oil on canvas.

The Edward Joseph Gallagher III Memorial Collection,
Gift of Edward Joseph Gallagher Jr., 1954.

43

Who doesn't (Heart) music?
Tickling ivories and strumming chords,
Blaring brass and soaring flutes,
Rhythmic guiro and tapping drum,
There is so much music to hear.

* . * ° . * ° . ° ° . ° ° .

The Woodshed

1969, by **ROMARE BEARDEN**. American. Cut and pasted printed and colored papers, photostats, cloth, graphite, and sprayed ink on Masonite.

Dancing in Colombia

1980, by **FERNANDO BOTERO**. Colombian. Oil on canvas.

Anonymous Gift, 1983. © Fernando Botero.

Two Young Girls at the Piano

1892, by AUGUSTE RENOIR. French. Oil on canvas.

Robert Lehman Collection, 1975.

Marble seated harp player

2800–2700 BCE. Cycladic. Marble.

Rogers Fund, 1947.

A Musical Party

detail, 1659, by GABRIËL METSU.
Dutch. Oil on canvas.

Marquand Collection, Gift of Henry G.
Marquand, 1890.

Merengue en Boca Chica

1983, by **RAFAEL FERRER**. American (born Puerto Rico).
Oil on canvas.

Purchase, Anonymous Gift, 1984. © Rafael Ferrer.

Woman with a Lute

c. 1662–63, by **JOHANNES VERMEER**. Dutch. Oil on canvas.

Bequest of Collis P. Huntington, 1900.

Drum

early twentieth century. Akan Ashanti people. Wood, polychrome, skin, trade beads, and plastic.

Gift of Raymond E. Britt Sr., 1977.

Circus Sideshow (Parade de cirque)

1887–88, by **GEORGES SEURAT**. French.

Oil on canvas.

Bequest of Stephen C. Clark, 1960.

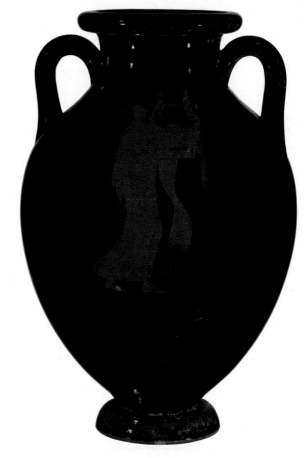

Terracotta amphora (jar)

c. 490 BCE, attributed to the Berlin Painter. Greek. Terracotta; red-figure.

Fletcher Fund, 1956.

Watercolor of musician playing sona

late eighteenth century. Chinese. Watercolor on paper.

Gift of Lawrence Creshkoff, 1990.

Cowboy Singing

c. 1892, by **THOMAS EAKINS**. American.
Watercolor and graphite on off-white wove paper.
Fletcher Fund, 1925.

The Love Song

1868–77, by **SIR EDWARD BURNE-JONES**. British. Oil on canvas.

The Alfred N. Punnett Endowment Fund, 1947.

A Lady Playing the Tanpura

c. 1735. India. Ink, opaque and transparent watercolor, and gold on paper.

Fletcher Fund, 1996.

I (HEART)

Singing and Dancing

Who doesn't (Heart) to sing and dance?

Choral music and sultry tones,

Tapping toes and swaying skirts,

Cheek to cheek and wheeling jig,

There are so many ways to sing and dance.

Man and woman dancing

c. 1890–1910, by **JOSÉ GUADALUPE POSADA** or **MANUEL MANILLA**. Mexican. Metal plate engraving.

The Elisha Whittelsey Collection, The Elisha Whittelsey Fund, 1946.

Three Girls Singing and Dancing

c. 1815, by **KUBO SHUNMAN**. Japanese. Part of an album of woodblock prints (surimono); ink and color on paper.

H. O. Havemeyer Collection, Bequest of Mrs. H. O. Havemeyer, 1929.

74

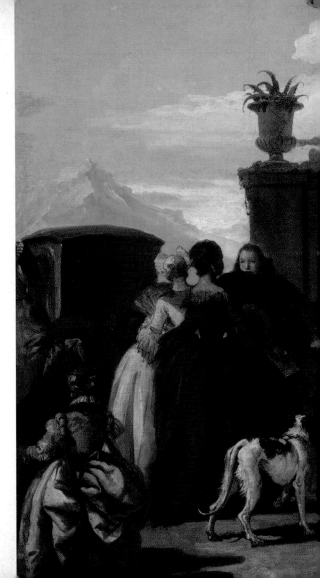

A Dance in the Country

c. 1755, by **GIOVANNI DOMENICO TIEPOLO**. Italian. Oil on canvas.

Gift of Mr. and Mrs. Charles Wrightsman, 1980.

76

Spanish Music Hall

1902, by **EVERETT SHINN**. American.
Oil on canvas board.

Bequest of Miss Adelaide Milton de Groot
(1876–1967), 1967.

The Organ Rehearsal

1885, by **HENRY LEROLLE**. French.

Oil on canvas.

Gift of George I. Seney, 1887.

Nasturtiums with the Painting "Dance" I

1912, by **HENRI MATISSE**. French. Oil on canvas.

"Dancing Dervishes", Folio from the Shah Jahan Album

recto: c. 1610,
by MIR 'ALI HARAVI.
Attributed to India. Ink,
opaque watercolor, and
gold on paper.

Purchase, Rogers Fund and
the Kevorkian Foundation Gift,
1955.

84

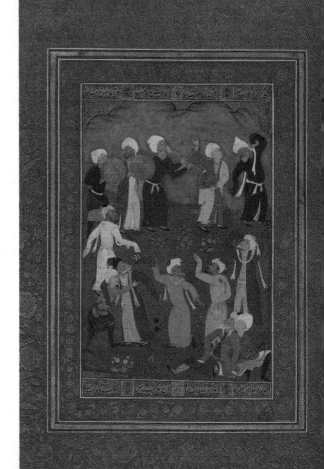

Soldier Playing the Theorbo

1865, by ERNEST MEISSONIER. French. Oil on wood.

Bequest of Martha T. Fiske Collord, in memory of her first husband, Josiah M. Fiske, 1908.

85

[Couple Dancing at Club El Morocco, New York City]

c. 1955, by **GARRY WINOGRAND**.
American. Gelatin silver print.

John B. Turner Fund, 1986. © The Estate of
Garry Winogrand, courtesy Fraenkel Gallery, San
Francisco.

The Rehearsal of the Ballet Onstage

c. 1874, by **EDGAR DEGAS**. French. Oil colors freely mixed with turpentine, with traces of watercolor and pastel over pen-and-ink drawing on cream-colored wove paper, laid down on bristol board and mounted on canvas.

H. O. Havemeyer Collection, Gift of Horace Havemeyer, 1929.

Who doesn't (Heart) to read, write, and draw?

Books and journals or paper and canvas,

Pens and pencils or paints and brushes,

Facts and fictions or landscapes and portraits.

There is so much to read, write, and draw!

I (HEART)

Reading, Writing, and Drawing

Russians Reading and Writing

1861, by UTAGAWA YOSHIKAZU. Japanese.

Polychrome woodblock print; ink and color on paper.

Gift of Lincoln Kirstein, 1959.

Reading the Scriptures

detail, 1874, by **THOMAS WATERMAN WOOD**. American. Watercolor, gouache, and graphite on light tan wove paper.

Rogers Fund, 1966.

A Woman Reading

detail, 1869 and 1870, by **CAMILLE COROT**. French. Oil on canvas.
Gift of Louise Senff Cameron, in memory of her uncle, Charles H. Senff, 1928.

Young Woman Writing Calligraphy

1793, by **KUBO SHUNMAN**. Japanese.
Polychrome woodblock print (surimono);
ink and color on paper.

Purchase, Marjorie H. Holden Gift, 2012.

The Interior of an Atelier of a Woman Painter

detail, 1789, by MARIE VICTOIRE LEMOINE. French. Oil on canvas.

Gift of Mrs. Thorneycroft Ryle, 1957.

The Writing Master

detail, 1882, by THOMAS EAKINS. American. Oil on canvas.

John Stewart Kennedy Fund, 1917.

99

In the Generalife

1912, by **JOHN SINGER SARGENT**. American.
Watercolor, wax crayon, and graphite on white
wove paper.

Purchase, Joseph Pulitzer Bequest, 1915.

Cover for 'Coleccion de Cartas Amorosas Cuaderno No. 6', a young woman writing a letter at a desk

c. 1900, by JOSÉ GUADALUPE POSADA. Mexican. Photo-relief and letterpress on green paper.

The Elisha Whittelsey Collection, The Elisha Whittelsey Fund, 1946.

The Beginning

detail, one of three panels, 1946–49, by **MAX BECKMANN**. German. Oil on canvas.

Marie Joséphine Charlotte du Val d'Ognes

detail, 1801, by **MARIE DENISE VILLERS**. French. Oil on canvas.

Mr. and Mrs. Isaac D. Fletcher Collection, Bequest of Isaac D. Fletcher, 1917.

Reading at a Table

1934, by **PABLO PICASSO**. Spanish. Oil on canvas.

107

I (HEART)
Animals

Who doesn't (Heart) animals?

Grazing deer and growling tigers,

Leaping fish and splashing frogs,

Barking dogs and scrambling cats,

There are so many animals in the world!

Air: 24 Hours, Five P.M.

1991–92, by **JENNIFER BARTLETT**. American. Oil on canvas.

Rabbits on a Log

1897, by ARTHUR FITZWILLIAM TAIT.
American (born England). Oil on canvas.

Gift of Mrs. J. Augustus Barnard, 1979.

Panel with striding lion

c. 604–562 BCE.
Babylonian. Ceramic
and glaze.

Fletcher Fund, 1931.

Weight in shape of frog

c. 2000–1600 BCE. Babylonian. Diorite or andesite.

Purchase, Leon Levy and Shelby White Gift,
Rogers Fund and Nathaniel Spear Jr. Gift, 1988.

Charge of the Light Brigade, Cawston Ostrich Farm, South Pasadena, California, No. 9116

c. 1905. American. Photochrom.

The Jefferson R. Burdick Collection, Gift of Jefferson R. Burdick.

Deer amid pine trees

detail, nineteenth century. Korean. Two hanging scrolls, ink and color on silk.

Purchase, Friends of Asian Art Gifts, 2013.

Camel

first half of twelfth century (possibly 1129–34). Spanish. Fresco transferred to canvas.

The Cloisters Collection, 1961.

A Limier Briquet Hound

c. 1856, by **ROSA BONHEUR**. French. Oil on canvas.

Catharine Lorillard Wolfe Collection, Bequest of Catharine Lorillard Wolfe, 1887.

The Innocent Eye Test

1981, by **MARK TANSEY**.
American. Oil on canvas.

Gift of Jan Cowles and Charles
Cowles, in honor of William S.
Lieberman, 1988.
© Mark Tansey.

Bark Painting

1940s–50s, by
BRYYINYUWUY
(possibly). Ingura people.
Bark, paint.

The Michael C. Rockefeller
Memorial Collection, Bequest of
Nelson A. Rockefeller, 1979.

Snowy Landscape

nineteenth century, by **KUBO SHUNMAN**. Japanese.
Polychrome woodblock print (surimono); ink and color on paper.

Crocodile Rattle

eighth century. Mayan. Ceramic.

The Michael C. Rockefeller Memorial Collection,
Bequest of Nelson A. Rockefeller, 1979.

133

34 – 31

Monkey

1884, by **GEORGES SEURAT**. French. Conté crayon.

Bequest of Miss Adelaide Milton de Groot (1876–1967), 1967.

Spring Play in a Tang Garden

eighteenth century. Chinese. Handscroll; ink and color on silk.

From the Collection of A. W. Bahr, Purchase, Fletcher Fund, 1947.

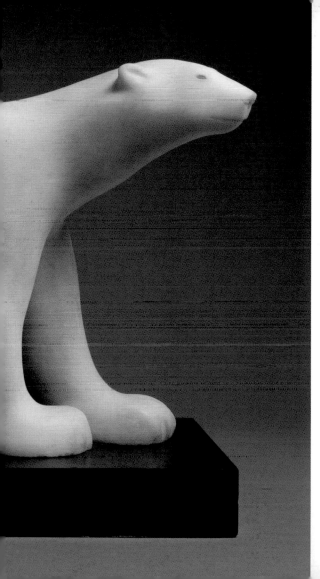

Polar Bear

c. 1923, by **FRANÇOIS POMPON**. French.
Marble on marble base.

Purchase, Edward C. Moore Jr. Gift, 1930.

139

Tiger and Cubs

c. 1884, by JEAN-LÉON GÉRÔME.
French. Oil on canvas.

Bequest of Susan P. Colgate, in memory of her
husband, Romulus R. Colgate, 1936.

Hippopotamus ("William")

c. 1961–1878 BCE. Egyptian. Faience.

Gift of Edward S. Harkness, 1917.

The Horse Fair

detail, 1852–55, by ROSA BONHEUR. French. Oil on canvas.

Gift of Cornelius Vanderbilt, 1887.

Who doesn't (Heart) family?

Loved ones nearby and loved ones far off,

Sons and daughters and brothers and sisters,

Moms and dads and neighbors and friends,

There are so many ways to be a family!

I (HEART)

Family

"The Emperor Shah Jahan with his Son Dara Shikoh", Folio from the Shah Jahan Album

recto: c. 1530–50, painting by **NANHA**, calligraphy by **MIR 'ALI HARAVI**. Attributed to India. Ink, opaque watercolor, and gold on paper. Margins: Gold and opaque watercolor on dyed paper.

Purchase, Rogers Fund and The Kevorkian Foundation Gift, 1955.

Ernesta (Child with Nurse)
1894, by CECILIA BEAUX. American. Oil on canvas.

Maria DeWitt Jesup Fund, 1965.

Mother-and-Child Doll

1870–80. Seneca. Corn husk, cotton, wool, Native-tanned skin, glass, and silk.

Ralph T. Coe Collection, Gift of Ralph T. Coe Foundation for the Arts, 2011.

The Monet Family in Their Garden at Argenteuil

1874, by **ÉDOUARD MANET**. French.
Oil on canvas.

Bequest of Joan Whitney Payson, 1975.

The Van Moerkerken Family

c. 1653–54, by GERARD TER BORCH THE YOUNGER. Dutch.
Oil on wood.

The Jack and Belle Linsky Collection, 1982.

Mother and Son

c. 1769, by **SUZUKI HARUNOBU**. Japanese. Polychrome
woodblock print; ink and color on paper.

Purchase, Joseph Pulitzer Bequest, 1918.

Rubens, His Wife Helena Fourment, and Their Son Frans

detail, c. 1635, by
PETER PAUL RUBENS.
Flemish. Oil on wood.

Gift of Mr. and Mrs. Charles
Wrightsman, in honor of Sir
John Pope-Hennessy, 1981.

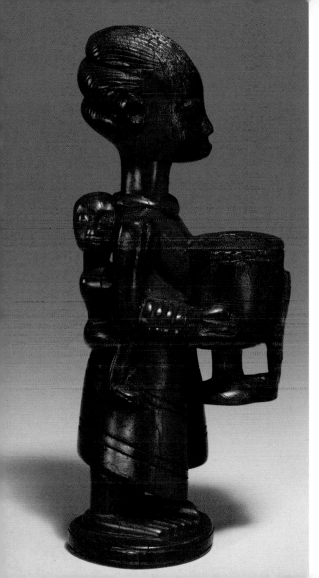

Figure: Mother with Vessel and Child

nineteenth to twentieth century. Yoruba peoples (Nigeria). Ivory.

Gift of Mr. and Mrs. Klaus G. Perls, 1991.

159

F. Luis Mora.
NAVAJO FAMILY

Navajo Family

c. 1928, by **F. LUIS MORA**. American (born Uruguay).
Graphite on wove paper.

Gift of Mr. and Mrs. Walter C. Crawford, 1979.

First Steps, after Millet

detail, 1890, by
VINCENT VAN GOGH.
Dutch. Oil on canvas.

Gift of George N. and
Helen M. Richard, 1964.

162

Hermine A.   Marie A.

Hermine and Marie Antoine

1850s–60s, by **FRANZ ANTOINE**. Austrian. Albumen silver print from glass negative.

David Hunter McAlpin Fund, 1948.

Madame Georges Charpentier (Marguérite-Louise Lemonnier) and Her Children, Georgette-Berthe and Paul-Émile-Charles

1878, by **AUGUSTE RENOIR**. French. Oil on canvas.

Catharine Lorillard Wolfe Collection, Wolfe Fund, 1907.

I (HEART)

Locomotion

Who doesn't (Heart) to be on the go?

Planes in air and boats at sea,

Trains on tracks and cars on roads,

Shoes on sidewalks and bikes on paths,

There are so many ways to go!

[Ship's Prow]

1950s–60s, by **WALKER EVANS**. American. Tempera on paper.

Walker Evans Archive, 1994.
© Walker Evans Archive, The Metropolitan Museum of Art.

171

America Today

detail, one of ten panels, 1930–31, by **THOMAS HART BENTON**. American. Egg tempera with oil glazing over Permalba on a gesso ground on linen mounted to wood panels with a honeycomb interior.

Gift of AXA Equitable, 2012.

Railroad Bridge over the Marne at Joinville

1871–75, by **ARMAND GUILLAUMIN**.
French. Oil on canvas.

Robert Lehman Collection, 1975.

Faience Tablet

c. 1400–1390 BCE.
Egyptian. Faience.
Gift of J. Pierpont Morgan, 1917.

Evening Calm, Concarneau, Opus 220 (Allegro Maestoso)

1891, by **PAUL SIGNAC**.
French. Oil on canvas.

Robert Lehman Collection, 1975.

The Bicyclist

1951, by FERNAND LÉGER. French. Oil on canvas.

The Mr. and Mrs. Klaus G. Perls Collection, 1997.
© 2019 Artists Rights Society (ARS), New York / ADAGP, Paris.

Cessna C-145

early twentieth century. American, collector card from the Airplanes of America series (D2), issued by the Kelley Baking Company to promote Kelley's Bread. Commercial color lithograph.

The Jefferson R. Burdick Collection, Gift of Jefferson R. Burdick.

"Kai Khusrau Crosses the Sea", Folio from a Shahnama (Book of Kings) of Firdausi

c. 1610, by ABU'L QASIM FIRDAUSI. Attributed to India. Ink, opaque watercolor, and gold on paper.
Gift of Wendy Findlay, 1982.

Picture of a Balloon

1860, by MIYAGI GENGYO. Japanese.

Polychrome woodblock print; ink and color on paper.

Gift of Lincoln Kirstein, 1960.

Rush Hour, Fifth Avenue, New York

c. 1953, printed c. 1970, by **ANDREAS FEININGER**.
American (born France). Gelatin silver print.

Gift of the artist, 1971. Andreas Feininger / The LIFE Picture Collection / Getty Images.

The Green Car

1910, by **WILLIAM JAMES GLACKENS**. American. Oil on canvas.

Arthur Hoppock Hearn Fund, 1937.

O'P

[Vintage Car Sign]

collected 1960s–70s. Paint on ferrous metal.

Walker Evans Archive, 1994. © Walker Evans Archive,
The Metropolitan Museum of Art.

Skeletons (calaveras) riding bicycles

c. 1900, by **JOSÉ GUADALUPE POSADA.** Mexican. Etching on zinc.

Gift of Jean Charlot, 1930.

193

Boys in a Dory

1873, by **WINSLOW HOMER**. American. Watercolor washes and gouache over graphite underdrawing on medium rough textured white wove paper.

Bequest of Molly Flagg Knudtsen, 2001.

194

Who doesn't (Heart) the country?
Crops in the fields and big red barns,
Fields of flowers and forests of trees,
Mountains up high and waters below,
There is so much to see in the country.

I (HEART) THE
Country

The Harvesters

1565, by **PIETER BRUEGEL THE ELDER**. Netherlandish. Oil on wood.

Rogers Fund, 1919.

Spring Blossoms, Montclair, New Jersey

c. 1891, by **GEORGE INNESS**. American. Oil and crayon or charcoal on canvas.

Gift of George A. Hearn, in memory of Arthur Hoppock Hearn, 1911.

Winter Scene in Moonlight

1869, by **HENRY FARRER**. American.
Watercolor and gouache on white
wove paper.

Purchase, Morris K. Jesup Fund, Martha and
Barbara Fleischman, and Katherine and Frank
Martucci Gifts, 1999.

Mont Sainte-Victoire

c. 1902–6, by PAUL CÉZANNE. French. Oil on canvas.

IFUTALI

Urutaú

1983, by **JOSÉ GAMARRA**. Uruguayan. Oil on canvas.

Purchase, Anonymous Gift, 1983. © José Gamarra.

Woodstock Barn

1935–40, by **DAYTON BRANDFIELD**.
American. Serigraph.

Purchase, Harris Brisbane Dick Fund, 1940.

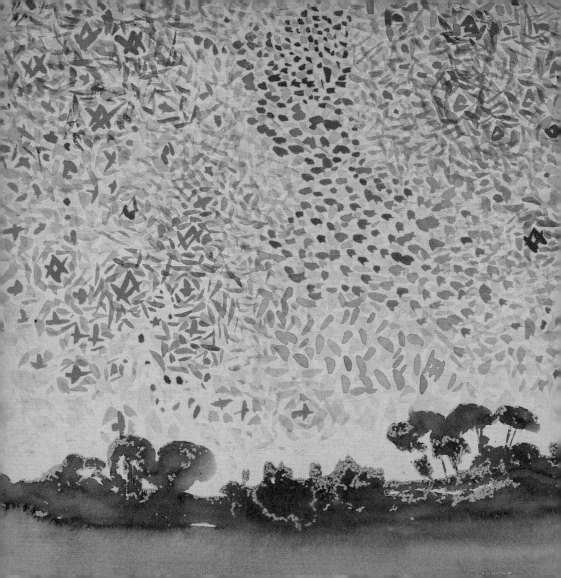

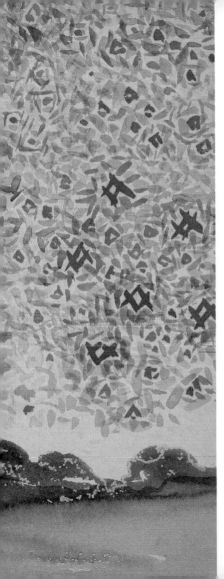

Landscape with Stars

c. 1905–8, by **HENRI-EDMOND CROSS**. French.
Watercolor on white wove paper.
Robert Lehman Collection, 1975.

Winter Landscape with Skaters on a Frozen Canal

detail, n.d., by **VINCENT JANSZ VAN DER VINNE.** Dutch. Watercolor over black chalk.

Purchase, Katherine Mondadori Gift, 2002.

212

Birds in a Landscape

detail, mid-eighteenth century. Attributed to India. Ink, opaque watercolor, silver, and gold on paper.

Gift of Richard Ettinghausen, 1975.

Sunrise on the Matterhorn

after 1875, by **ALBERT BIERSTADT**. American. Oil on canvas.

Gift of Mrs. Karl W. Koeniger, 1966.

Bamboo in the Four Seasons

attributed to **TOSA MITSUNOBU**, late fifteenth to early sixteenth century. Japanese. One of a pair of six-panel screens; ink, color, and gold leaf on paper.

The Harry G. C. Packard Collection of Asian Art, Gift of Harry G. C. Packard, and Purchase, Fletcher, Rogers, Harris Brisbane Dick, and Louis V. Bell Funds, Joseph Pulitzer Bequest, and the Annenberg Fund Inc. Gift, 1975.

217

Sunset

detail, c. 1850, by **EUGÈNE DELACROIX**. French.

Pastel on blue laid paper.

Gift from the Karen B. Cohen Collection of Eugène Delacroix, in honor of Philippe de Montebello, 2014.

219

Little River Farm

detail, 1979, by **YVONNE JACQUETTE**. American. Oil on canvas.

Gift of Dr. and Mrs. Robert E. Carroll, 1982. © Yvonne Jacquette.

Autumn Color

c. 1910, by **MARSDEN HARTLEY.** American. Oil on paperboard.

Anonymous Gift, in memory of Robert Glenn Price, 1954.

Wisconsin Landscape

1938–39, by JOHN STEUART CURRY. American. Oil on canvas.

George A. Hearn Fund, 1942.

Who doesn't (Heart) the city?

Soaring skyscrapers and spanning bridges,

Stores and shops and vendors and parks,

Honking horns and flashing lights,

There is so much to see in the city!

The Garden of the Tuileries on a Winter Afternoon

1899, by CAMILLE PISSARRO.
French. Oil on canvas.

Gift of Katrin S. Vietor, in loving memory
of Ernest G. Vietor, 1966.

Cubiculum (bedroom) from the Villa of P. Fannius Synistor at Boscoreale

detail, c. 50–40 BCE. Roman. Fresco.

Rogers Fund, 1903.

Seventh Avenue and 16th Street, New York

1932, by **MARK BAUM**. American. Oil on canvas.

Edith C. Blum Fund, 1983. © Mark Baum.

Chance Encounter at 3 A.M.

detail, 1984, by **RED GROOMS**. American. Oil on canvas.

Purchase, Mr. and Mrs. Wolfgang Schoenborn Gift, 1984. © Red Grooms.

235

East River from the Shelton Hotel
detail, 1928, by GEORGIA O'KEEFFE. American. Oil on canvas.

Alfred Stieglitz Collection, Bequest of Georgia O'Keeffe, 1986.

Ka'ba Tile

detail, c. 1720–30, by **OSMAN IBN MEHMED**. Turkish.
Stonepaste; polychrome painted under transparent glaze.

Gift of John and Fausta Eskenazi, in memory of Victor H. Eskenazi, 2012.

Brooklyn Bridge

c. 1912, by **JOHN MARIN**. American. Watercolor and charcoal
on paper.

Alfred Stieglitz Collection, 1949.

Regent Street, London

1906, by **ANDRÉ DERAIN**.

French. Oil on canvas.

The Lafayette

1927, by **JOHN SLOAN**. American. Oil on canvas.

Gift of The Friends of John Sloan, 1928. © 2019 Delaware Art
Museum / Artists Rights Society (ARS), New York.

Scenes in and around the Capital

detail, one of a pair, seventeeth century, unknown artist. Pair of six-panel folding screens; ink, color, gold, and gold leaf on paper.

Mary Griggs Burke Collection, Gift of the Mary and Jackson Burke Foundation, 2015.

247

Spring Morning in the Heart of the City

1890, reworked 1895–99, by **CHILDE HASSAM**.
American. Oil on canvas.

Gift of Ethelyn McKinney, in memory of her brother, Glenn Ford
McKinney, 1943.

The Block

1971, by **ROMARE BEARDEN**. American. Cut and pasted printed, colored and metallic papers, photostats, graphite, ink marker, gouache, watercolor, and ink on Masonite.

I (HEART)
Art

I (Heart) the **Index**

Note: Page numbers in *italics* refer to illustrations.

The Metropolitan Museum of Art is the largest museum in the Western Hemisphere and the world's most encyclopedic art museum. Founded in 1870, the Museum embraces more than two million works of art spanning five thousand years of world culture, from prehistory to the present, in all artistic media, and at the highest levels of creative excellence.

Library of Congress Cataloging-in-Publication Data
Names: The Metropolitan Museum of Art (New York, N.Y.), author.
Title: I (heart) art: work we love from The Metropolitan Museum of Art / [by the
Metropolitan Museum of Art].
Description: New York: Abrams Books For Young Readers, 2019. | Includes index.
Identifiers: LCCN 2018022204 | ISBN 978-1-4197-3387-1 (hardcover pob)
Subjects: LCSH: Art—New York (State)—New York—Juvenile literature. | Art—Themes,
motives—Juvenile literature. | Metropolitan Museum of Art (New York, N.Y.)—Juvenile
literature.
Classification: LCC N610.A555 I2 2019 | DDC 709.747—dc23

Book design by Katie Benezra

Cover image: *Marie Joséphine Charlotte du Val d'Ognes*, detail, 1801, by Marie
Denise Villers. French. Oil on canvas. Mr. and Mrs. Isaac D. Fletcher Collection,
Bequest of Isaac D. Fletcher, 1917.

Printed and bound in China
10 9 8 7 6 5 4 3 2 1

Abrams Books for Young Readers are available at special discounts when purchased
in quantity for premiums and promotions as well as fundraising or educational use.
Special editions can also be created to specification. For details, contact
specialsales@abramsbooks.com or the address below.

ABRAMS The Art of Books
195 Broadway, New York, NY 10007
abramsbooks.com